GLOBAL EFFECTS

THE IMPACT OF SCIENCE, TECHNOLOGY, AND ECONOMICS IN AUSTRALIA AND THE PACIFIC REALM

J.M. KLEIN

PowerKiDS press

Published in 2021 by The Rosen Publishing Group, Inc.
29 East 21st Street, New York, NY 10010

First Edition

Editor: Siyavush Saidian
Book Design: Tanya Dellaccio

Photo Credits: Cover Boy_Anupong/Moment/Getty Images; p. 4 stellalevi/E+/Getty Images; p. 7 Jonathan Clark/Moment/Getty Images; p. 9 andersen_oystein/E+/Getty Images; p. 11 Education Images/Universal Images Group/Getty Images; p. 13 (top) Apexphotos/Moment/Getty Images; p. 13 (bottom) ChameleonsEye/Shutterstock.com; p. 15 Shmenny50/iStock/Getty Images; p. 17 TriggerPhoto/E+/Getty Images; p. 19 (top) howamo/Shutterstock.com; p. 19 (bottom) Global_Pics/E+/Getty Images; p. 21 (top) TORSTEN BLACKWOOD/AFP/Getty Images; p. 21 (bottom) Auscape/Universal Images Group/Getty Images; p. 23 Dianne Manson/Getty Images News/Getty Images; p. 25 ullstein bild/Getty Images; pp. 27 (both), 29 Bloomberg/Getty Images.

Cataloging-in-Publication Data
Names: Klein, J.M.
Title: The impact of science, technology, and economics in Australia and the Pacific Realm / J.M. Klein.
Description: New York : PowerKids Press, 2021. | Series: Global effects | Includes glossary and index.
Identifiers: ISBN 9781725322561 (pbk.) | ISBN 9781725322585 (library bound) | ISBN 9781725322578 (6 pack) | ISBN 9781725322592 (ebook)
Subjects: LCSH: Australia–Juvenile literature. | Oceania–Juvenile literature. | Technology–Australia.| Science–Australia.
Classification: LCC DU96.K545 2021 | DDC 994–dc23

Manufactured in the United States of America

CPSIA Compliance Information: Batch #CSPK20: For Further Information contact Rosen Publishing, New York, New York at 1-800-237-9932

CONTENTS

ISLAND ECONOMIES

Stretching over the world's largest ocean, the many island nations of the Pacific realm have beautiful scenery. These countries also feature many **diverse** economies.

Australia and New Zealand are modern, **industrialized** countries. Australia is among the world's top economies as measured by **gross domestic product (GDP)**. In 2018, Australia had the world's 13th-largest GDP of about $1.4 trillion. New Zealand was 53rd in the world with a GDP of $204 billion.

Elsewhere, the majority of the islands throughout the Pacific Ocean depend on tourism, fishing, and agriculture. They also have much lower GDPs. Papua New Guinea had the region's third-highest GDP at $23 billion in 2018. Fiji's GDP was $5.5 billion. Tuvalu, a small country of nine coral islands, was one of the lowest at just $42 million.

INDUSTRIALIZED: HAVING A LOT OF ECONOMIC DEVELOPMENT.

THE LIFE EXPECTANCY GAP

Life expectancy, which measures how long an average person in an area lives, can show a country's economic and technological strength. More money and better technology help people live longer, healthier lives. As wealthy countries, Australia and New Zealand have high life expectancies. Australia's average is 82 years, and New Zealand's is 81 years. The region's less wealthy nations have lower life expectancies. Tonga's average is 77 years, while Nauru, Papua New Guinea, Tuvalu, and Kiribati are all under 70

ATOLL: A CIRCULAR-SHAPED ISLAND THAT HAS FORMED FROM A CORAL REEF.

AUSTRALIA IS A WEALTHY COUNTRY, AND ITS ECONOMIC SUCCESS IS REFLECTED IN THE ADVANCED AND BUSTLING CITY OF SYDNEY.

FAST FACT

A COUNTRY'S GDP PER CAPITA, OR PER PERSON, IS MEASURED BY DIVIDING ITS GDP BY ITS POPULATION. AUSTRALIA LEADS THE REGION WITH A GDP PER CAPITA OF $53,000. KIRIBATI, A COUNTRY OF 33 **ATOLLS** AND ISLANDS, HAS ONE OF THE LOWEST PER CAPITA GDPS AT JUST $1,700.

GDP (IN MILLIONS OF DOLLARS) AS OF 2017

AUSTRALIA	1,390,000	PALAU	321
FEDERATED STATES OF MICRONESIA	329	PAPUA NEW GUINEA	21,810
FIJI	5,054	SAMOA	844
KIRIBATI	186	SOLOMON ISLANDS	1,273
MARSHALL ISLANDS	199	TONGA	437
NAURU	114	TUVALU	40
NEW ZEALAND	200,800	VANUATU	837

THE GDPS OF THE PACIFIC REALM RANGE FROM THE WEALTHY COUNTRIES OF AUSTRALIA AND NEW ZEALAND TO POORER SMALL ISLAND COUNTRIES LIKE TUVALU.

MARKET ECONOMIES AND REGULATIONS

Today, many islands throughout the Pacific realm have market economies. That includes Australia and New Zealand. This means consumers set prices of goods and services—not the government. Prices go up because of supply and demand, not because of government **regulations**. Private companies compete for profit. Individuals and companies are allowed to own private property.

Economies like this still have government regulations. The amount of regulations varies between countries. Australia and New Zealand have free market economies where the government sets few regulations. In Fiji, the government controls and has a **monopoly** on sugar, its most important crop.

Australia and New Zealand are ranked in the top five countries of the world in terms of economic freedom. It's considered easy to open and run businesses in both countries.

FAST FACT

SUGAR PRODUCTION USED TO BE FIJI'S MOST IMPORTANT INDUSTRY, BUT ITS TOURISM AND CLOTHING BUSINESSES HAVE EXPANDED IN THE 21ST CENTURY.

NEW ZEALAND'S LIGHT REGULATIONS HAVE HELPED CITIES, SUCH AS AUCKLAND, BECOME BUSY BUSINESS CENTERS.

DEREGULATING NEW ZEALAND

New Zealand's government used to pass strict regulations on its economy. These rules stopped prices from increasing too much, especially during wartime. In the 1980s, however, New Zealand's economy declined, and the government removed many of the rules. New Zealand's economy is now one of the most open economies in the world. Today, New Zealand's biggest challenge for economic growth is its small population. Fewer than 5 million people live in the country, making it one of the world's smallest developed countries.

TRADITIONAL ECONOMIES AND COMMUNITY OWNERSHIP

While the economies of islands throughout the Pacific are changing, many islands still have features of a **traditional economy**. Historically, communities have worked together to survive and grow food.

In many of the region's island nations, land is owned by the community. In Papua New Guinea, tribal groups own 95 percent of the country's land, which is covered in forests. Some foreign companies have **negotiated** with native landowners for the rights to sell their eucalyptus, rosewood, and pine. Others, however, have taken advantage of tribal landowners and illegally harvested wood on their land.

Since 1874, laws in Fiji have not allowed land to be owned by non-native Fijians. About 90 percent of the land in Fiji is owned by native groups called *mataqali*. Farmers of other **ethnic** groups **lease** land from the *mataqali*.

TRADITIONAL ECONOMY: GENERALLY REFERS TO AN ECONOMY BASED ON SUBSISTENCE FARMING OR CUSTOMARY ACTIVITIES.

NEGOTIATE: TO DISCUSS SOMETHING IN ORDER TO MAKE AN AGREEMENT.

FAST FACT

TOURISM BROUGHT CASH ECONOMIES TO PLACES LIKE SAMOA, WHERE NATIVE PEOPLES NOW EXCHANGE GOODS AND SERVICES FOR MONEY INSTEAD OF **BARTERING**.

PAPUA NEW GUINEA IS COVERED IN RICH FORESTS. TRIBAL CLANS OWN MOST OF THE LAND, AND 85 PERCENT OF PEOPLE GROW THEIR OWN FOOD TO SURVIVE.

DIFFERENT WAYS OF OWNING LAND

The Maori, **aboriginal** people in New Zealand, traditionally owned land **communally**. During its years of **colonialism**, the British took land from the Maori. Today, some of the land has been returned to its original owners. All the land in Tonga belongs to the monarchy, but it's divided among the nobility. At the age of 16, male Tongans receive an area of land to raise crops, thus continuing Tonga's traditional economic practices.

ABORIGINAL: AN ADJECTIVE THAT DESCRIBES ANYONE FROM AN INDIGENOUS GROUP ANYWHERE IN THE WORLD, OR SPECIFICALLY, A MEMBER OF THE INDIGENOUS ABORIGINAL PEOPLES OF AUSTRALIA.

ISLAND AGRICULTURE

Islands in the Pacific realm used to be self-sufficient. People would fish, farm, or raise livestock to feed themselves, their families, and their communities. They didn't rely on international investment or business.

Increasing technology has made Pacific islands more economically dependent on outside countries, but many islands still look to their roots in **subsistence farming** and fishing. Most people grow food and fish as ways to feed their families, not to sell. Papua New Guinea has fertile, or rich, farmland, and isolated communities don't have large markets. About 85 percent of people rely on growing their own food.

Farming is important to **indigenous** families in places like Fiji, where people grow enough coconuts, cocoa, kava, taro, pineapples, cassava, and bananas to feed their families. They may sell anything left over to make extra money.

INDIGENOUS: DESCRIBING GROUPS THAT ARE NATIVE TO A PARTICULAR REGION.

SUBSISTENCE FARMING: FARMING THAT FOCUSES ON FEEDING ONE'S FAMILY OR COMMUNITY INSTEAD OF ON TRADE.

FAST FACT

IN ESPECIALLY SMALL NATIONS LIKE THE FEDERATED STATES OF MICRONESIA, VANUATU, AND TUVALU, SUBSISTENCE FARMING IS STILL THE MOST WIDESPREAD AGRICULTURAL ACTIVITY.

MORE THAN HALF OF PAPUA NEW GUINEA'S FEMALE WORKERS ARE IN AGRICULTURE, WHICH IS BY FAR THE MOST IMPORTANT INDUSTRY IN THE COUNTRY.

THE AGRICULTURE INDUSTRY THROUGHOUT THE PACIFIC REALM

Agriculture is central to the economy of many Pacific islands. Bananas, sugarcane, and a root plant called kava are grown throughout the region. Coconuts are widespread on almost every island. In Samoa, agriculture provides jobs for almost two-thirds of the workforce and makes up 40 percent of the GDP. In Fiji, sugar is a key crop. Pineapple and sugar used to be more important to Hawaii, but the island state still harvests both in large amounts. Tonga is known for its vanilla and squash.

FARMING AND LIVESTOCK IN AUSTRALIA AND NEW ZEALAND

As the driest continent in the world, Australia has some of the worst land for growing crops, especially in the **outback**. Technology has been a major **adaptation** for Australian agricultural workers. For example, farmers can use drones to check on livestock. Sensors tell them how much water and fertilizer to give to crops.

Australian farmers grow enough food to meet 90 percent of the country's demand. Australia also provides almost 15 percent of the world's wheat products and is a major sugar exporter. In addition to farming, Australia produces the most wool in the world. More than half of the land in the country is pastureland, meaning it's used for livestock.

Climate change is a threat to Australian agriculture. The land quality is becoming worse and the available water is decreasing.

ADAPTATION: AN ADJUSTMENT TO THE SURROUNDING CONDITIONS.

OUTBACK: THE ARID INLAND AREAS OF THE AUSTRALIAN CONTINENT.

FAST FACT

MANY RURAL AREAS IN AUSTRALIA ARE AT RISK OF BUSHFIRES. IN 2019 AND 2020, AN ESPECIALLY DAMAGING FIRE SPREAD ACROSS NEW SOUTH WALES. IT KILLED LIVESTOCK AND DESTROYED HOMES, WHICH WILL HARM THE COUNTRY'S FARMING PRODUCTION.

RAISING AND GROWING IN NEW ZEALAND

In New Zealand, there are more than six sheep to every person. The country's farming and livestock industries are significant contributors to the overall economy. Dairy products, meat, wool, wheat, apples, corn, and barley are some of the country's major **exports**. As New Zealand's economy becomes more developed, agriculture is becoming less important. In 2017, farming and livestock made up 5.7 percent of the country's GDP and only employed 6.6 percent of workers.

EXPORT: A GOOD THAT IS SOLD TO ANOTHER COUNTRY.

SHEEP OUTNUMBER PEOPLE IN NEW ZEALAND, BUT MODERN TECHNOLOGY IS REDUCING THE IMPORTANCE OF AGRICULTURE IN THE COUNTRY.

FISHING INDUSTRY BENEFITS AND CHALLENGES

The commercial fishing industry is important to Pacific realm economies. Fish is a significant export in many countries. In Fiji, products made from fish make up 10 percent of the money earned through exports.

However, a lack of fishing equipment, such as large boats, makes it hard for many islands to fish on a large scale. Foreign countries fishing in the Pacific realm catch more than $2 billion worth of tuna each year. In contrast, Pacific island countries only catch about $600 million worth of tuna per year.

To prevent overfishing, New Zealand puts limits, called quotas, on fishing. New Zealand's Maori own about 50 percent of the country's quotas. Other countries are trying to put similar quotas in place to protect their fishing industries.

FAST FACT

INSTEAD OF FISHING THEMSELVES, MANY PACIFIC COUNTRIES BRING IN MONEY BY SELLING FISHING LICENSES TO FOREIGN COUNTRIES OR COMPANIES.

AQUACULTURE AND AUSTRALIA

Australia has a small fishing industry compared to the size of its coastline. Many fish live in the Great Barrier **Reef**, which could be damaged by large amounts of fishing. The narrow **continental shelf** surrounding Australia makes the water too warm for some fish, and it also makes pulling fishing nets behind boats difficult. Fishers in Australia and other islands use **aquaculture** to raise fish in fishing holes. Many modern practices are based on techniques used by indigenous people for hundreds of years.

REEF: A CHAIN OF ROCKS OR CORAL, OR A RIDGE OF SAND, AT OR NEAR THE WATER'S SURFACE.

CONTINENTAL SHELF: A PORTION OF A CONTINENT THAT IS SUBMERGED UNDER THE OCEAN AND GRADUALLY SLOPES AWAY FROM THE CONTINENT.

AQUACULTURE SYSTEMS LIKE THIS ARE USED TO RAISE AND FARM FISH IN AUSTRALIA AND OTHER PACIFIC ISLANDS.

THE IMPORTANCE OF TOURISM

Beautiful beaches and other local attractions draw millions of visitors to Australia and the Pacific realm every year, making tourism a leading economic activity throughout the region.

Places like Tahiti and Bora Bora in French Polynesia are major tourist destinations. In Australia, tourism is a $143 billion industry. More than 9 million tourists came to Australia in 2018. Tourism is the main economic activity in places like Fiji, Palau, American Samoa, Hawaii, the Northern Mariana Islands, and Guam.

Tourism is an industry with a lot of potential. Its value in the region's economy could increase even more. However, it costs a lot of money to build hotels and airports for tourists. Not every country is able to spend money to develop the **infrastructure** needed to further increase tourism.

TOURISM IS A LEADING ECONOMIC ACTIVITY IN AUSTRALIA AND THE PACIFIC REALM. THE COVID-19 GLOBAL PANDEMIC, OR WIDESPREAD ILLNESS, THAT BEGAN IN 2019 IMPACTED TOURISM AND OTHER MAJOR INDUSTRIES IN THE REGION AND AROUND THE WORLD.

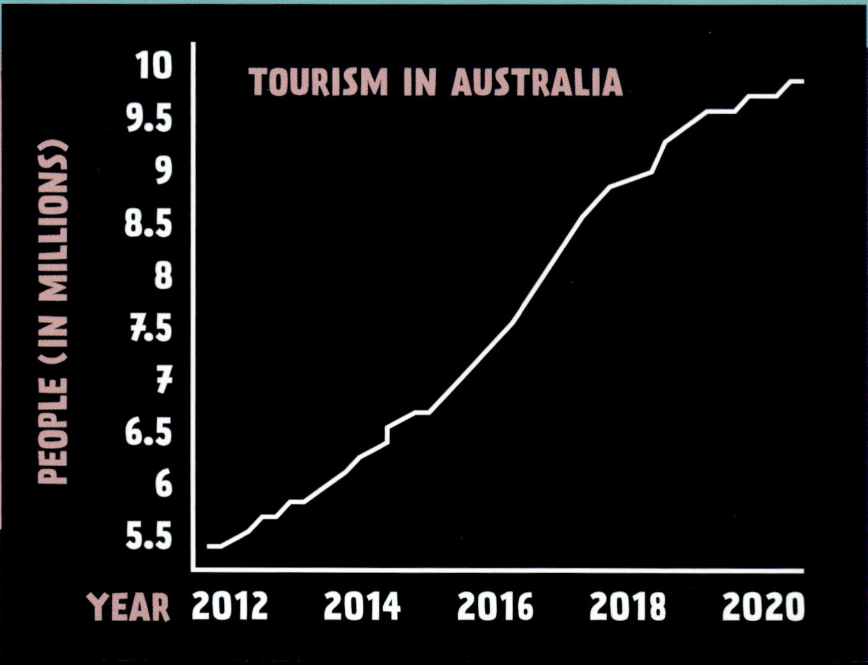

FAST FACT

THE AMERICAN *LORD OF THE RINGS* FILMS SIGNIFICANTLY INCREASED TOURISM TO NEW ZEALAND, WHERE THE MOVIES WERE FILMED. FANS CAN BOOK TOURS OF THE FILM'S RECOGNIZABLE LOCATIONS.

FRENCH POLYNESIA'S BORA BORA HAS MANY LOCATIONS AT WHICH TOURISTS CAN STAY IN UNIQUE LOCAL STRUCTURES, LIKE THESE OVERWATER BUNGALOWS.

ADVENTURE TOURISM

New Zealand received 3.8 million tourists in 2018. While other countries have beaches and swimming, New Zealand is proud of its adventure tourism. Brave tourists can zip-line, skydive, raft, or go jet boating. The less adventurous can kayak, ski, or cycle at many locations across the country. People in New Zealand created the first bungee jump business in 1988. Leaping from bridges, cliff edges, and stadium roofs around the country is now a popular activity for many thrill-seeking tourists.

JOBS AND THE SERVICE INDUSTRY

As with most modern advanced economies, the **service industry** is important to the economy of Australia and New Zealand. This field includes jobs in finance, health care, education, the government, housing, and construction.

The service industry dominates Australia's economy. It makes up three-quarters of Australia's GDP and is now more important than agriculture, mining, and **manufacturing**. Three-quarters of the Australian workforce are employed in service jobs, including the 5 percent who work in tourism.

A large portion of New Zealand's population used to work in agriculture, but service industries have increased alongside technological advances. Today, service industries employ two-thirds of the workforce, mainly in tourism, banking, and insurance.

The service industry also dominates the economy in Hawaii, where tourism and government jobs are widespread.

SERVICE INDUSTRY: BUSINESSES THAT PROVIDE LABOR-INTENSIVE WORK RATHER THAN MAKING A PRODUCT.

MANUFACTURING: BUSINESSES THAT PRODUCE CONSUMER PRODUCTS.

FAST FACT

GOVERNMENTS ARE MAJOR EMPLOYERS IN SOME PARTS OF THIS REGION, INCLUDING AMERICAN SAMOA, PALAU, AND THE FEDERATED STATES OF MICRONESIA.

MADE UP OF MORE THAN 340 CORAL ISLANDS, PALAU HAS BEAUTIFUL BEACHES AND WORLD-FAMOUS DIVING SPOTS. SO MANY TOURISTS COME TO PALAU THAT IT OVERWHELMS THE SERVICE INDUSTRY.

PALAU AND THE IMPACT OF TOURISM

Increased tourism has affected the service industry in Australia and the Pacific realm—sometimes harming some of the smaller island countries. In Palau, tourism is responsible for creating about half of its yearly GDP. The country's white sand beaches and world-famous diving spots attract around 120,000 tourists each year. There are only 20,000 Palauans, which makes it hard to keep up as tourism expands. The large number of tourists has also caused environmental damage.

NATURAL RESOURCES AND MINING

Mining is important on some islands in the Pacific realm. Most of those islands are **continental islands**, which have more natural resources.

Papua New Guinea mines gold, copper, silver, and coal. Oil is its main export. New Caledonia, a French territory, has 25 percent of the world's nickel resources. The islands of New Caledonia used to rely on subsistence farming and fishing, but nickel mining is expected to draw increasing international business. This foreign investment should make life easier for people living there, but some are worried mining will harm the environment.

Mines in Australia produce copper, iron, and sapphires. It's also the world's leading source of opals. Other natural resources include oil, coal, and natural gas. Gold, coal, and natural gas are major products of New Zealand.

CONTINENTAL ISLAND: AN ISLAND FORMED BY TECTONIC PLATE MOVEMENT THAT CAUSES THE RISING AND FOLDING OF THE OCEAN FLOOR.

FAST FACT

ISLANDS LIKE SAMOA, WHERE ALMOST HALF THE LAND IS COVERED BY TREES, HAVE FEW NATURAL RESOURCES. INSTEAD, THESE COUNTRIES HARVEST TIMBER, AN IMPORTANT NATURAL RESOURCE.

PHOSPHATE MINING ONCE MADE NAURU VERY WEALTHY, BUT THE GOVERNMENT DIDN'T PREPARE FOR THE INDUSTRY'S DECLINE.

PHOSPHATE HIGHS AND LOWS

The small island country of Nauru used to have a lot of minerals called phosphates, which can be used in many industries. Mining this mineral once made Nauru very wealthy. In the 1960s and 1970s, Nauru's per capita GDP was among the world's highest. Now, however, the island's phosphate is almost gone, and Nauru is one of the world's poorest countries. This is an example of the dangers of a country's economy relying too heavily on a single product.

MANUFACTURING AND INCOME SOURCES

In mid–20th century Australia, manufacturing made up more than 30 percent of the national GDP. Since then, numbers have fallen, and just over 10 percent of the country's modern GDP comes from the industry. One-third of manufacturing in Australia is controlled by foreign businesses.

In New Zealand, most manufacturing takes the form of processing agricultural products. This means taking basic materials, such as wool, and turning them into usable products. The country produces a lot of **textiles**, carpets, beverages, and chemicals. As sugar production has declined in Fiji, the garment industry has expanded. This manufacturing field has added jobs and helped the economy of the island.

Some of the region's smaller islands also participate in manufacturing. For example, Samoa makes coconut products like creams and oils. A Japanese-owned manufacturing plant is Samoa's second-biggest employer.

FAST FACT

MOST PEOPLE WHO LIVE IN AUSTRALIA AND THE PACIFIC REALM ARE YOUNG. THE AVERAGE AGE IN THE REGION IS ABOUT 33.

WORKERS ARE SHOWN HERE OPENING OYSTERS AT A NEW ZEALAND FACTORY. MUCH OF THE COUNTRY'S MANUFACTURING COMES FROM THE PROCESSING OF AGRICULTURE PRODUCTS.

GRANTS AND U.S. CONNECTIONS

Foreign countries, such as the United States, often provide much-needed money and support to Pacific islands. For example, the Marshall Islands receives **subsidies** from the United States in exchange for land that's used in missile testing. A U.S. connection is also important to many other islands. Guam is home to a U.S. military base. In Samoa, the United States is the main employer. Guam and Samoa are U.S. territories. Hawaii is an American state, and its economy receives important revenue and jobs from the nation's military.

ECONOMIC INTERDEPENDENCE

The islands throughout the Pacific are economically connected, and they often depend on one another. Many of the islands rely on trade with their neighbors to get important resources, including food. In Samoa, for example, even though the majority of jobs are in agriculture, there's still not enough food grown for the number of people living there.

Nauru's 20th-century mining harmed the land and made farming difficult. The country now relies on other countries—mainly Australia—for food and water. Most food in the Federated States of Micronesia is also **imported**.

Fiji imports both food—including rice, meat, and fish—and business resources, such as machinery and chemicals. However, relying on other countries for necessary goods can be risky, so the island is trying to reduce its dependence on imported food.

FAST FACT

ISLANDS LIKE FIJI AND PAPUA NEW GUINEA MUST IMPORT FUEL, MACHINES, AND EQUIPMENT. THIS DRIVES UP THE COST OF BUSINESS DEVELOPMENT AND CONSTRUCTION.

LARGE SHIPPING CRAFT LIKE THIS COMMONLY SAIL BETWEEN ISLANDS IN THE PACIFIC REALM, OFTEN CARRYING IMPORTANT RESOURCES.

MONEY SENT HOME

A significant source of **capital** in some Pacific islands is the money sent home from relatives who are working in places like the United States and New Zealand. These are called **remittances**. Remittances make up more than 15 percent of household income in Samoa. People in Tuvalu, Tonga, the Solomon Islands, Fiji, and Vanuatu also rely on these payments. **Migrant** workers in Australia send home more than $16 billion per year.

CAPITAL: A REGION'S FINANCIAL VALUE, BASED ON PRODUCTS THEY MANUFACTURE, INCLUDING THE FACILITIES USED TO MAKE AND STORE THOSE PRODUCTS.

INTERNATIONAL TRADE

International trade is a major part of most economies in Australia and the Pacific realm. Australia's exports make up more than 15 percent of its GDP. Natural gas and mined materials, like coal and gold, are the country's major exports. Fruit and vegetables grown in Australia are popular in North America during its winter off-season. Each year, Australia's exports feed 36.6 million people worldwide.

Australia has been successful internationally because it has many free-trade agreements with other countries. These agreements make business easier, allowing companies to invest in job growth and product development.

Smaller Pacific islands often sell specialty or luxury items. For example, French Polynesia exports 90 percent of the pearls it produces, and this single product makes up nearly 70 percent of the territory's export income.

FAST FACT

AUSTRALIA HAS STRONG TRADING PARTNERSHIPS WITH MOST OF THE ISLANDS IN THE PACIFIC. AUSTRALIA'S PARTNERSHIP WITH NEW ZEALAND IS ESPECIALLY CLOSE AND THE TWO SUPPORT EACH OTHER.

NEW ZEALAND IS AMONG THE TOP DAIRY EXPORTERS IN THE WORLD. IT ALSO EXPORTS OTHER PRODUCTS LIKE WOOL AND PROCESSED CHEESE.

DISTANCE TO TRADING PARTNERS

Most countries in Australia and the Pacific realm are far away from allies and trading partners. This can sometimes make trade difficult. Australia and New Zealand have close ties with the United States, Canada, and Great Britain, all of which are thousands of miles away. This distance makes it expensive to ship goods, whether imported or exported. Both Australia and New Zealand have been working to strengthen trade relationships with their Asian neighbors, which are much closer.

SCIENCE, TECHNOLOGY, AND THE FUTURE

Although some might think Australia and the Pacific realm are not on the cutting edge of technology, **innovation** in the region has contributed to developments in technology and science. For example, Wi-Fi technology was an Australian creation in the 1990s. In the 21st century, inventors from New Zealand have come up with a working jetpack and a car that works on both land and sea. Australian computer scientists helped develop the technology that would become Google Maps.

Though Australia and the Pacific realm are far away from most other countries, they have a lot to offer the world. From modern inventions to unique tourism opportunities, this region produces valuable goods and offers unique services. As these islands become more connected to the rest of the world, their economies will continue to grow.

INNOVATION: A NEW OR BETTER WAY OF DOING SOMETHING.

FAST FACT

ANCIENT INHABITANTS OF SMALLER PACIFIC NATIONS CAME UP WITH MANY TECHNOLOGICAL BREAKTHROUGHS, INCLUDING NAVIGATION SYSTEMS TO SAIL BETWEEN ISLANDS.

AUSTRALIA IS HOME TO THE COMMONWEALTH SCIENTIFIC AND INDUSTRIAL RESEARCH ORGANIZATION (CSIRO), A LARGE AGENCY THAT STUDIES CLIMATE, ARTIFICIAL INTELLIGENCE, HEALTH, FARMING, AND MANY OTHER TOPICS.

ENVIRONMENTAL RESEARCH

Scientists in the Pacific realm are world leaders in environmental research. The region is considered to be highly at risk from climate change because of rising sea levels, which threaten many islands. The area is also close to Antarctica's **ozone** layer hole. Solar power development and sustainable resource management are key areas of research and innovation in this region. Additionally, scientists in Fiji are trying to develop floating cities and New Zealand researchers are working to reduce methane gas from cows.

OZONE: THE GASEOUS LAYER AROUND THE EARTH'S ATMOSPHERE THAT BLOCKS HARMFUL RAYS FROM THE SUN.

GLOSSARY

aquaculture: The cultivation of fish or shellfish for food.

barter: To exchange goods or services in return for other goods or services.

colonialism: Control by one power over a dependent area or people.

communal: Shared or used by a community.

diverse: Different or varied.

ethnic: Describing a group that shares common cultural traits, such as language.

gross domestic product (GDP): The total value of the goods and services produced by the people of a nation.

imported: Brought into a country from somewhere else.

infrastructure: Basic equipment and structures like roads and bridges that are needed for a country to function properly.

lease: To grant temporary possession or use.

migrant: A person who goes from one place to another to find work.

monopoly: A situation in which only one company controls an industry or product.

regulation: An official rule or law that says how something should be done.

remittance: The sending of money to a recipient at a distance.

subsidy: Assistance or money given to someone to pay for the costs of something.

textile: A cloth-based product.

FOR MORE INFORMATION

BOOKS

Hamby, Rachel. *Restoring the Great Barrier Reef*. Lake Elmo, MN: Focus Readers, 2020.

Klepeis, Alicia. *Australia*. New York, NY: Cavendish Square Publishing, 2018.

McGhee, Karen. *Australia's Greatest Inventions*. Sydney, Australia: Bauer Media, 2016.

WEBSITES

Australia
www.australia.com
Students can learn more about Australia on the tourism website of Australia, which features lots of information about the country.

Australia Facts: Get Ready for the Lowdown Down Under!
www.natgeokids.com/au/discover/geography/countries/facts-about-australia
National Geographic Kids' website provides a wide variety of information about Australia.

Welcome to New Zealand
www.newzealand.com
New Zealand's tourism website offers information about the country and lots of pictures on an accessible website.

Publisher's note to educators and parents: Our editors have carefully reviewed these websites to ensure that they are suitable for students. Many websites change frequently, however, and we cannot guarantee that a site's future contents will continue to meet our high standards of quality and educational value. Be advised that students should be closely supervised whenever they access the internet.

INDEX